A BASIC GUIDE TO LETTERING

Page from an illuminated manuscript book. Written on vellum with illuminated initials.

A
BASIC
GUIDE TO
LETTERING

ROBERT D. BUCKLEY

CHILTON BOOK COMPANY
Philadelphia   New York · London

CONTENTS

INTRODUCTION

This book has been planned as a guide to the study of the basic fundamentals of letters and their proportions.

Its aim is to point out some of the difficulties that confront the beginner, and to suggest ways of overcoming them.

The diagrams and alphabets used throughout the book have not been presented with the view that no further study of lettering is needed. They are presented as a simplified method for the study of letter proportions, and for acquiring a better knowledge and facility in their rendering.

In the study of lettering, the student will find there are no quick and easy ways of learning to letter. The basic forms of the letters, their construction, and relative proportions are learned by observation and careful practice. In acquiring this knowledge, the student will find that the drawing of letters becomes almost an unconscious effort.

It is unreasonable to ask students to draw letters when the basic characteristics or features of the letter forms are not understood.

The measurements and suggestions presented here are the results of many years of observation, both as a commercial artist and teacher. They are as nearly correct as it is mathematically possible to indicate them, and are intended only as a guide to better understanding of letter construction.

The Roman forms used as models throughout the book have been accepted as standards of good letter forms for centuries. Of all letters, their legibility and pleasing designs have been the most enduring.

As the history of lettering is not within the scope of this book, no attempt will be made to cover that subject, except in reference to or explanation of the classification of letter forms.

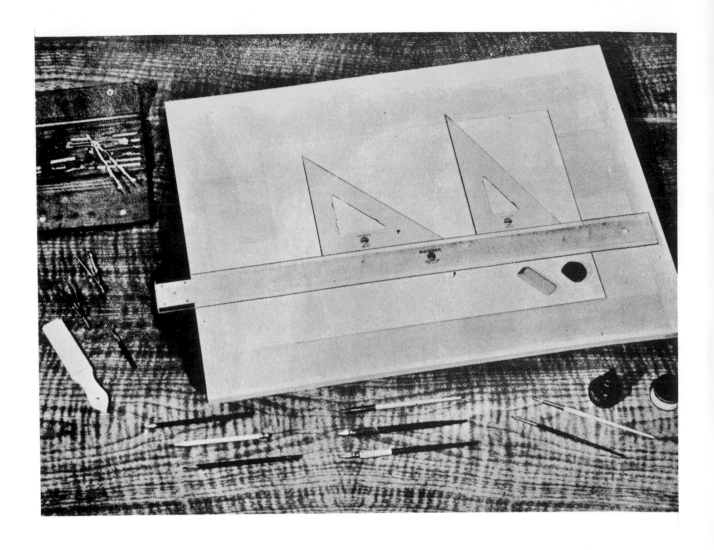

INTRODUCTORY REMARKS

The tools and materials you will need for learning to letter consist of a drawing board, paper, pencils, pens and holders, black ink, suitable erasers, art gum or kneaded rubber eraser. To this list you should add a T-square and triangles. A desirable addition to the above items is a set of mechanical drawing instruments. This set will contain dividers, and the necessary bow compasses for both pencil and ink.

Paper used for finished work should have a hard surface suitable for pen and ink rendering. It will be a matter of preference whether you choose a smooth surface or one with a slight "tooth".

As a start, it is recommended that you use tracing paper. This kind of paper is sold in blocks of various sizes and is excellent for practice work.

For drawing, use a B or HB pencil. The harder pencils, H or 2H, are used for tracing or for drawing guide lines. A sandpaper block is helpful in forming and maintaining a good point.

A variety of pens is available for lettering; the student should select those best suited to his needs. A square-cut steel pen, Hunt's Speedball series C-2 and C-3, will be necessary for drawing the practice strokes and roman letters described in the book. These pens come in a variety of sizes, each size making a different thickness of line.

Fine pointed pens, such as Gillott's 290, 291 and 170, are a few of the many good pens recommended for your use.

A pen should be cleaned thoroughly after using. Ink left in a pen will harden and spread the nibs, making the pen unfit for further use. An ordinary piece of cloth will suffice as a pen wiper.

The ruling pen differs from the ordinary drawing pen. This pen is used for ruling mechanical lines of even thickness and is drawn against a T-square or triangle for this purpose. The ruling pen is filled with either a pen or brush and is never dipped into the bottle of ink. The sides of this pen must be kept clean and free of ink to avoid blotting. Ink compasses are filled in the same manner as the ruling pen.

When starting to work, sit comfortably with the light source at the left. Hold the pencil lightly as you would for ordinary writing and never apply any great pressure.

Learn to draw in pencil first, because it allows mistakes in drawing or spacing to be corrected easily.

Don't try to be original at first — just copy the forms as outlined until you have mastered them completely. The first attempts will not be satisfactory, but with practice and perseverance you will eventually be able to draw good letter forms.

Lettering must usually fit a given space. The letters should first be sketched in lightly with a pencil for approximate spacing. Top and bottom guide lines are then drawn to the proper height of the letters.

After the letters are sketched in and the spacing established, it will be well for you to pencil in accurately the details of each letter before finishing them in ink.

In beginning the study of lettering, you should understand some of the terms as used throughout the book.

The ends of the strokes for many styles of letters may be finished with a terminal or serif. The appearance of a letter may be changed by the character of these terminals or serifs (see page 34).

Letters may be changed by varying the thickness of the stroke. This is illustrated by the words "Light Face" and "Bold Face".

Other variations are shown by the words "Condensed" and "Letterspaced". Letterspacing is applied to capitals only, never to lower case or italics.

The variations in alphabets are endless, but study of the basic forms is essential in pursuing the artistic possibilities of letters.

THIS IS KNOWN AS A SANS SERIF LETTER

LIGHTFACE

THIS COPY IS SET IN ROMAN CAPITALS

CONDENSED

This is known as sans serif lower-case

This copy is set in

BOLDFACE

roman lower-case

this line is set in italic lower-case

THIS LINE IS LETTERSPACED

MAW

DQOGC

HNKTVUYXZ

BEFSLPR

IJ

BASIC
LETTER PROPORTIONS

To aid the student in the study of letters, and letter proportion, we have grouped the Roman capitals into four basic divisions, e.g. the circle, the square, the ¾ square and the ½ square.

This method of associating letter forms to specific areas will furnish the student with a concrete starting point. To illustrate the prescribed method, let us take for example the word BOSTON. (See Steps 1-4).

STEP 1. On a separate sheet of paper (a) construct the areas that contain the letters assigned to them, e.g. the circle, the square, the ¾ square and the ½ square.

On your work sheet (b) draw two parallel lines (c) the height of the shapes you have drawn.

Now slide sheet (a) on which you have drawn the circle, square, etc., underneath your work sheet. The top and bottom lines of the shapes will coincide with lines (c) on your work sheet.

STEP 2. The first letter of this assignment is the letter B. This letter is in the ½ square group. Move the ½ square area, which is on the sheet beneath, to the starting point of the word and in this area, on your work sheet, draw the letter B.

STEP 3. The next letter O is in the circle group. Slide the underneath paper, which has the circle drawn on it, into position next to the letter B and draw the letter O.

STEP 4. The next letter is S and is also in the ½ square group. Again, slide the underneath ½ square area into position and draw the letter S.

Using this procedure, draw the remaining characters in the word. Any word, or group of words, may be drawn using this same method.

It is suggested in this preliminary work that the student work on tracing paper. The reason for working on this paper is that the student may readily move his work about underneath the sheet he is working on and quickly make improvements or adjustments.

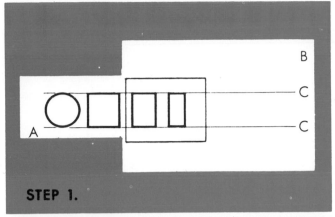

STEP 1.

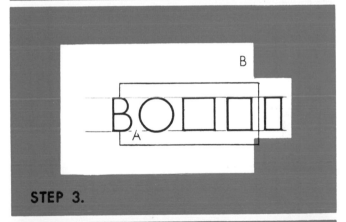

STEP 2.

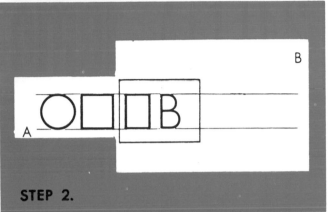

STEP 3.

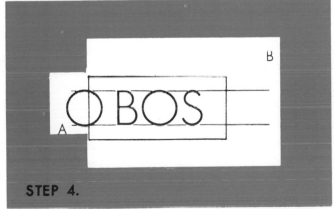

STEP 4.

SPACING

A letter seldom exists alone; therefore we must consider the word as the unit in letter design. The ability to draw fine letters does not always result in a pleasing word arrangement.

The optical effect of lines in relation to each other sometimes creates a disturbance to the eye. To offset these effects, we must arrange our letters or words in such a way that they are easy and pleasant to read. This is known as "spacing".

Experiments with a few combinations of letters will demonstrate that each combination creates a space difference in size and shape from every other combination. Therefore, it is obviously impractical to space letters by measuring off equal distances between each character.

Spacing is balance, not distance. To attain good balance it is necessary to consider the optical effect of the spaces between letters. Words and lines of letters must have an "even color". No white gaps or black masses must appear where the letters are too far apart or too close together. To accomplish this "even color", certain liberties may be taken with the form of the letters, such as shortening the cross bar of the T, or the lower bar of the L. A good test is to half close your eyes and notice if any open or heavy spots appear in the words.

Occasionally letters are spaced with more than the normal amount of spacing between each character. This practice is called "letterspacing".

a. LILAC

b. LILAC

FIG. 1. **(a)** To illustrate the error in spacing letters evenly, here is a word with all the letters spaced the same distance apart. It will be obvious that some of the letters are too far apart while others are too close.
(b) Word re-spaced with areas between letters having the optical appearance of being equal.

NE HO DO

FIG. 2. For the student accustomed to measuring distances, the following will be helpful in developing a sense of balance rather than distance between letters. Straight stemmed letters always seem closer together than curved letters; therefore this combination requires the most space between them. Straight stemmed letters and curves can be closer together. Two adjoining round letters can be very close to each other.

AY LV LA

FIG. 3. When A is followed or preceded by Y, the bottom of the A comes directly under the top of the Y. When L is followed by a slanted letter like V, the top comes directly over the end of the L. L and A present a difficult combination. As a solution, shorten up on the bottom stroke of the L to allow the A to be moved over very close.

AND NOW

FIG. 4. Spaces between words should be larger than those between letters within words. The width of the character "O" is often used as a guide to word spacing.

The student will find these hints helpful in acquiring a "feeling" for good spacing. In the final analysis, however, spacing by judgment of eye is the only method and this skill can be acquired by observation and intelligent practice.

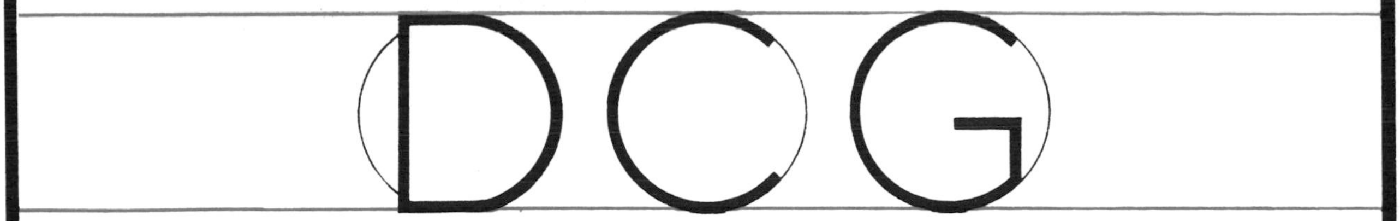

DCG

Although the D, C and G are to be thought of as being circular in form, note that these letters are cut back from the complete circle.

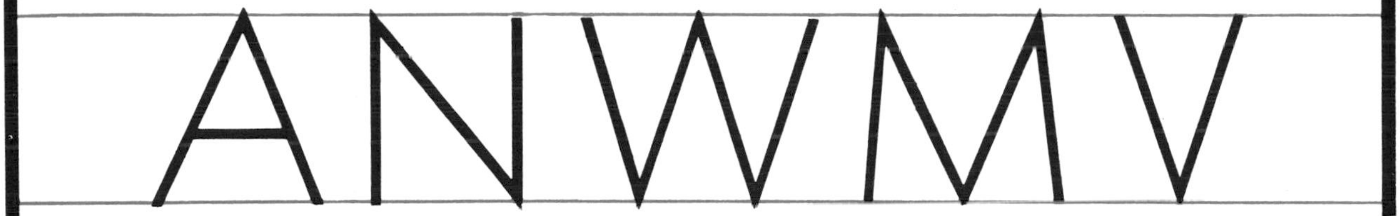

ANWMV

The points of these angular letters should extend slightly beyond the guide lines, to avoid appearing short.

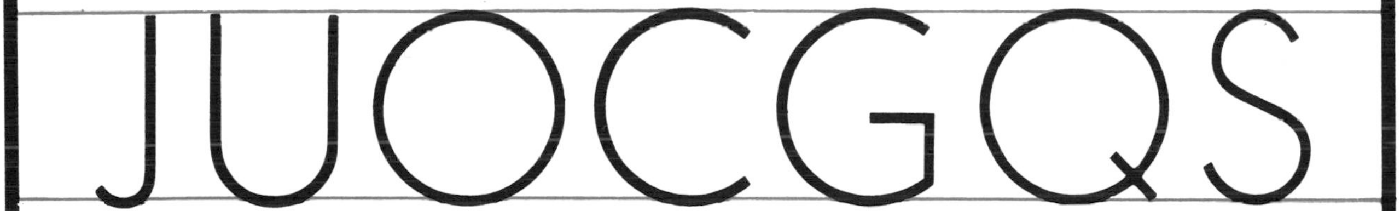

JUOCGQS

The circular parts of these letters should also extend through the top and bottom guide lines. Due to an optical illusion, these letters appear smaller if this provision is not made.

BKRXSZ

In constructing these letters it is better to draw the upper portion a trifle smaller than the lower. This is done to prevent the letter from appearing top heavy.

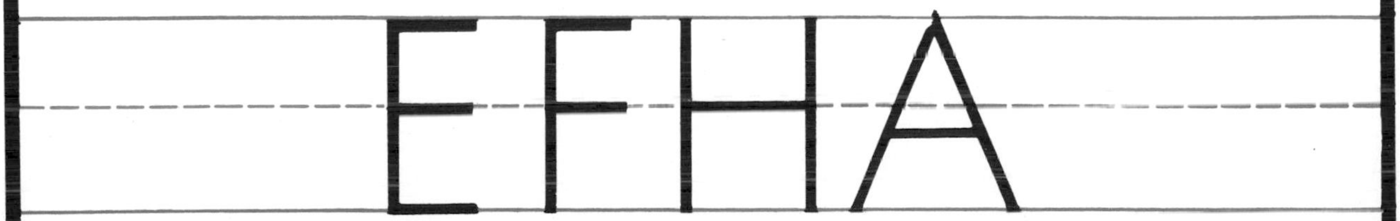

EFHA

The cross bars of these letters are drawn slightly above the actual center, with the exception of A, which is drawn slightly below.

ABCDEFGHIJKLM
NOPQRSTUVWX
YZ1234567890

ABCDEFGHIJKLM
NOPQRSTUVWX
YZ1234567890

ABCDEFGHIJKLM
NOPQRSTUVWX
YZ1234567890

This alphabet shows the various degrees of weight in which letters may be drawn. Note that the additional color is obtained by adding thickness to the inside of the letter. It is advisable in drawing heavier letters to have the pointed terminals of A, N, M, etc. meet the guide lines as shown in the second and third examples.

BONWIT TELLER
FIFTH AVENUE AT 56th STREET

AMERICAN CAN COMPANY

Lord Kitchener
AUTOMOBILE

STEAMSHIP
LINES

LOVELL PRESSURE CLEANSER

Pleasant Excursions

NATION
HOUSE

Span

Many pleasing type arrangements can be obtained by using letters of contrasting sizes and colors.

Letters may also be "inlined", or used in reverse color panels to achieve a different look.

The sans-serif italic letters closely resemble the upright letters in character. Due to the slant of the letters, the forms become more condensed and the circular forms become oval in shape.

It will be noted that these letters occupy approximately the same area as the upright letters. When they are slanted, any divisional lines appearing in the upright letter areas bear the same relation to the slanted letter areas.

The italic letters are not considered as readable as the more conventional upright forms; therefore, they are used sparingly in large masses.

One or several italic words in a line of upright words is an excellent use of this style for emphasis.

A B C D E F G H I J

K L M N O P Q R S

T U V W X Y Z & ?

a b c d e f g h i j k l m

n o p q r s t u v w x y z

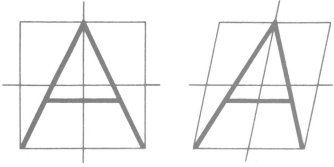

SANS SERIF LOWER CASE

All alphabets include capitals, and an equal number of corresponding small letters, called lower case.

Though the study of these forms will serve as an introduction to the Roman lower case letters, they, in themselves, possess a style and character known as gothic type.

This series of forms which we are to study, is a skeletonized Roman type, from which all non-essentials have been stripped. It is designed with geometric simplicity, its strokes are of uniform thickness and its curves and angles are drawn with exactness. It lacks serifs and can be identified by its geometrical appearance. Its simplicity is used expressively where emphasis, and a modern feeling are considerations.

Though these letters do constitute a particular style, our immediate concern is not one of style, but rather a study and understanding of the basic lower case forms. To familiarize the student with the basic forms, they have been classified into groups of similar proportions. These proportions are not followed as rigidly as in the case of the capitals, but rather are to be pictured mentally when drawing the various letters. For example, **think** of a circular form when constructing O, C, or any of the letters in the circular group. **Think** of the n, u or the h as being square in form. Following this process of **thinking** areas, visualize in your mind the area in which the letter belongs before actually drawing it.

FIGURE 1

The letters illustrated in the panels differ most in form from their capitals. As an aid in memorizing these forms, construct on a separate piece of paper, the letter a, as shown in Fig. 1. Slide this diagram of the letter a underneath the tracing paper on which you are working. You will readily see that the addition of ascenders or descenders to the diagram will form the g, d, and q. By reversing the diagram and adding a descender, the p is formed; by adding an ascender the b is formed.

FIGURE 2

The letters in panel three are fundamentally alike in construction. On a separate piece of paper draw the letter n, as shown in Fig. 2. Slide this diagram underneath your tracing paper (as you did with the diagram a). You will note that the addition of an ascender to the left hand side of the diagram forms the H, while the inverted form of the diagram makes the u. Two n's (slightly narrower in width than the diagram) form the m. The letters t and f are almost the inverted forms of each other, the t not equalling the f in height. The horizontal bars of these letters cross the upright on the main height of the other letters in the line. The lower case l is simply a vertical line as tall as the capitals.

The letter r is a straight line, drawn to the height of the main body of the letters, and has a slight curve at the top right hand side.

These letters follow the same form as their capitals, the only difference being that of size. The lower case s should be drawn more on the ellipse rather than following the circle. This will prevent the letter from appearing too narrow.

OCS XWVZ

k is the same as its capital, except that the upright is extended to form the ascender. With the exception of the dots, i and j are the same forms as their capitals. The form of the y is changed by continuing the right hand angular stroke to form a descender.

kijy

a changes in form in the lower case by becoming circular in shape. It has a straight upright on the right hand side of the letter. The lower case e is also circular in shape, and the cross bar cuts the letter in half. Letters of light weight are more graceful if the bar is drawn slightly higher.

ae

These are variants of the forms illustrated and follow the Roman in character. The bow of the a and the lower loop of the g should be elliptical, rather than round in appearance. If either of these forms is used, it should be used consistently throughout a sentence, or phrase.

ag

After careful study of the letter forms illustrated, you are now ready to begin drawing. Sketch in lightly on tracing paper the forms you are going to draw. Here on this paper you may use any guide lines, horizontal or vertical, that may help you in their construction. Here also you can make any corrections in spacing or in the thickness of the letters that you wish. You may even retrace your original start, altering and perfecting as you retrace. Too much stress can hardly be made regarding the importance of perfecting work on tracing paper. It shows exactly what the finished work will look like and leaves nothing to be corrected in the inking.

Having satisfied yourself that the drawing is as perfect as you can make it, trace it down on your drawing paper. First, rub over the back of the forms to be transferred with a soft pencil (4B); then go over the letters with a hard pencil (4H). After transferring the work to the drawing paper, it is advisable to go over the light pencil lines to straighten or strengthen them, and your work is now ready to be inked.

Although most fine lettering should be done free hand, the geometric style suggested here as your starting point, may be ruled quite successfully. Therefore, rule and compass all lines that lend themselves to this treatment. When you study and render the more difficult Roman forms, most of your drawing will be free hand.

Later, as will be explained, liberties in these basic proportions will be permissible and quite often desirable in order to inject character or style to the lettering.

In some phases of art, where so much depends upon the skill and creativeness of the artist, there can be no rigid set of rules. In lettering however, we are not creating new characters, but interpreting forms that were created centuries ago, and adapting them for present day use. Therefore we have established precedents to follow in lettering.

When the student has mastered these basic forms and their relative proportions and has acquired skill and judgment through his training, then he can safely experiment with changes in form and proportion.

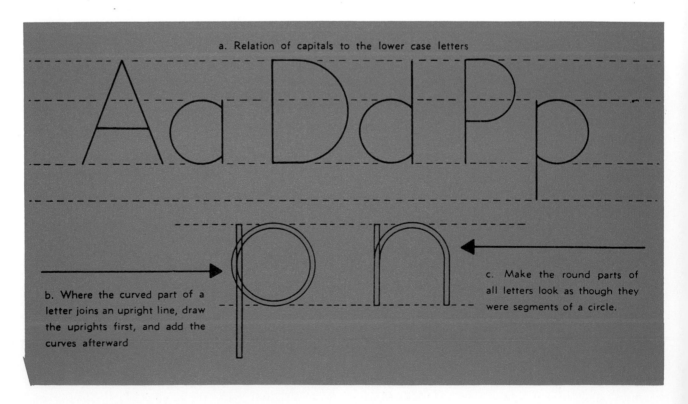

a. Relation of capitals to the lower case letters

b. Where the curved part of a letter joins an upright line, draw the uprights first, and add the curves afterward

c. Make the round parts of all letters look as though they were segments of a circle.

a b c d e f g h
i j k l m n o p q
r s t u v w x y z

a b c d e f g h
i j k l m n o p q
r s t u v w x y z

a b c d e f g h
i j k l m n o p q
r s t u v w x y z

Like the capitals of this style, the lower case letters can be drawn in varying weights to effect a particular tone or emphasis to the lettering. Thickness should be added to the inside of letters.

NUMERALS are drawn to match the design of the corresponding letters of any alphabet. In some styles, notably in the gothics, the curved sides are drawn straight to conform with the style of letter used. Italic numerals take the same slant as the letters they accompany, and may be drawn to any weight.

Considerable study and practice should be applied to the drawing of numerals — as one badly shaped numeral could spoil an otherwise perfect job. Care should be taken that they do not appear too black or heavy in pattern.

1 2 3 4 5 6 7 8 9 0

1 2 3 4 5 6 7 8 9 0

1 2 3 4 5 6 7 8 9 0

1 2 3 4 5 6 7 8 9 0

1 2 3 4 5 6 7 8 9 0

There are many designs of condensed sans serif letters that depart from the accepted Roman forms. The designs are pleasing in that fundamentally they retain the same relative proportions to one another. The E and S for example are still narrow while the M and W are usually the widest letters in the alphabet.

Sans serif letters may be drawn in many thicknesses, but any additional increase in weight should be added to the inside of the letters to avoid changing their character.

In nearly all weights it is advisable to draw the horizontals and diagonals slightly thinner than the vertical strokes. Unless this provision is made these strokes will appear heavier than the uprights. This optical effect is obvious in M and N where the diagonals meet the upright strokes.

In drawing the letters M, N, V, W, A, where there is a choice of using a flat or pointed terminal, be consistent by drawing all terminals in the same style. In X the lines cross at the optical center, and the base is slightly wider than the top.

The beginner will find the S one of the most difficult letters to draw. Time and study should be devoted to its construction. The design of the letter is based on two circles, the bottom circle being slightly larger. The knowledge of this construction will lessen the normal tendency to flatten the top and bottom of the letter.

It is a matter of personal choice as to finish of the ends. They may be finished off at angles or verticals. Whichever style is chosen, it must be consistent with similar endings on the C, G.

Despite the stiffness and mechanical look of these gothic types, they are popular, as can be proven by scanning the newspapers and magazines. Because of their directness, layout men favor them for putting emphasis into a display line.

A B C D E F G
H I J K L M N
O P Q R S T U
V W X Y Z & 1 2
3 4 5 6 7 8 9

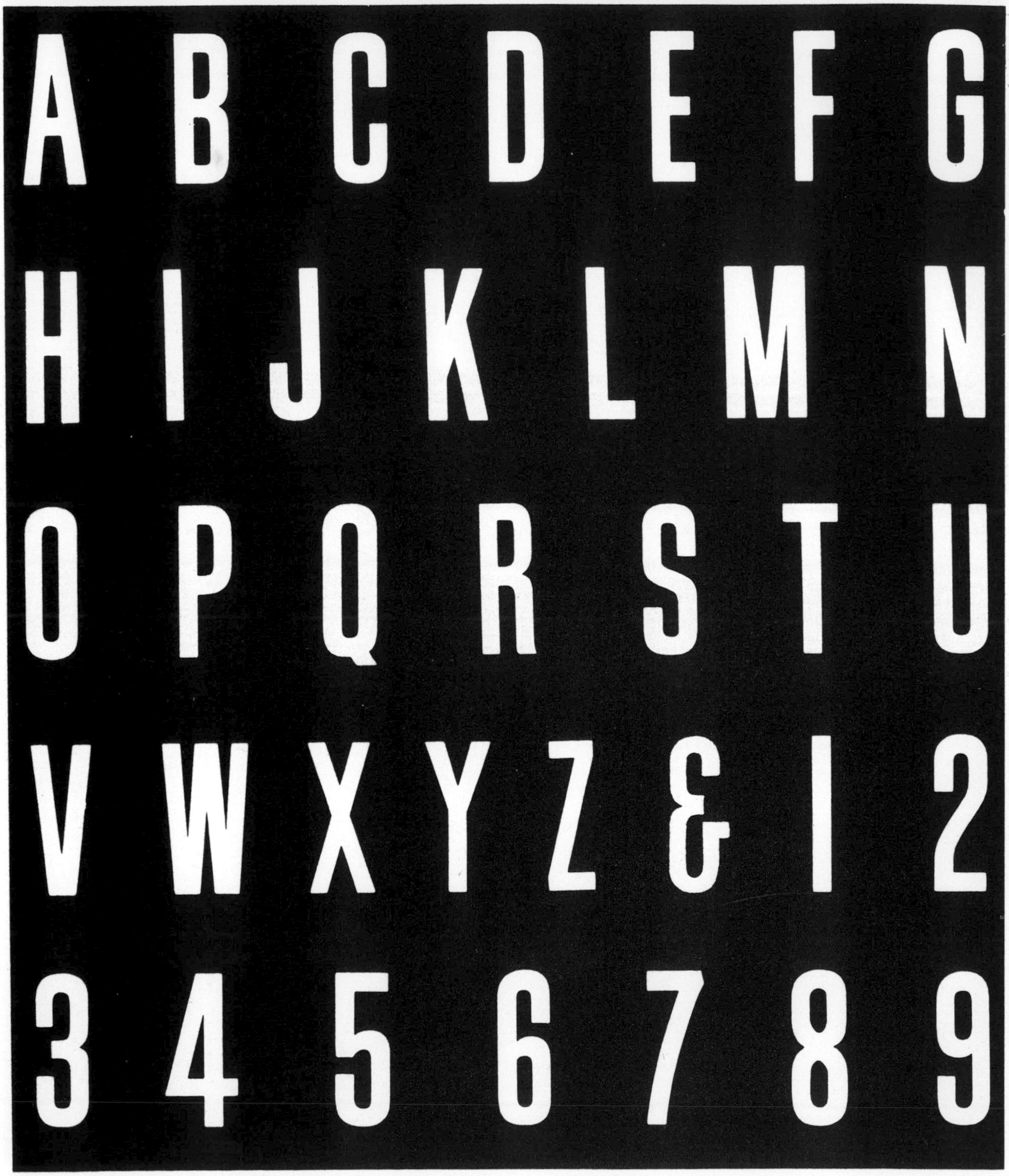

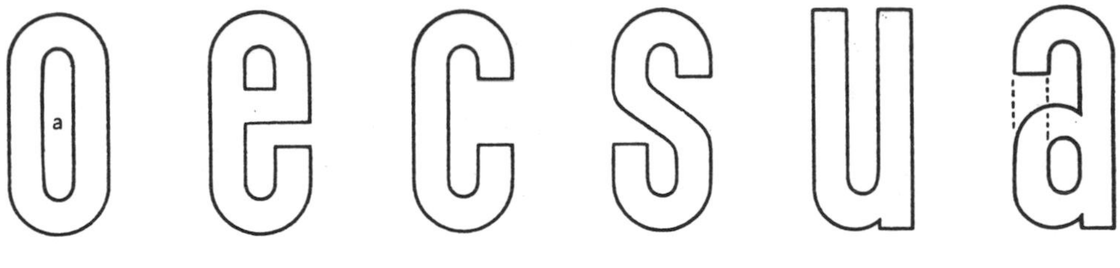

o e c s u a

Using the lower case O as a model, note how easy it is to construct many of the other letters of this alphabet. In the diagrams above, the dotted lines showing the original model have been drawn·to help the understanding of this method. In drawing this alphabet, the openings (a) of these areas must be alike in size.

a b c d e f g
h i j k l m n
o p q r s t u
v w x y z

ABCDEFG
HIJKLMNO
PQRSTUVW
XYZ&?!

abcdefghi
jklmnopqr
stuvwxyz

tough problems here!

YOUR FOOD MONEY!

dessert dish

SPUDNUT means fine

Satisfied Customer ALLIES

all eyes are on COLUMBIA

Examples of sans serif letters as used in present day advertising. These show only a few of the many combinations of weights and styles that are possible with this type of letter.

MAW

DQOGC

HNKTVUXYZ

BEFSLPR

IJ

28

FROM SANS SERIF TO ROMAN

In preceding chapters, we studied the Basic Proportions and structure of the Roman letters. For the basis of our study the letters were stripped of all non-essential parts, leaving only the basic skeleton forms.

To associate these forms with the finished Roman letters, we must bridge the gap between these forms of even thickness, and the built-up letters of varying weights and serifs. Previous to the invention of movable types, the recording of events was the result of laborious hand work. The implement or pen used in recording this information imparted certain natural characteristics to the letters. This natural character became the basis of design for all Roman types.

Since it was the nature of the pen that influenced these thick and thin forms, it is important that we realize that letters assumed their contours not by chance, but from the pen which fashioned them.

Assuming that the student will have a keener appreciation of letter forms, if he has a knowledge of their origin, our studies will follow the same pattern as exemplified in the Roman forms.

The early scribes used a quill, which was the natural writing implement of that time. Present day manufacturers have duplicated this writing quality in the form of a steel pen. This type of pen, properly handled, will simulate the various strokes of the quill, allowing us to effect the same qualities in our letters.

This method produces letters which are the models for construction. These models are often modified and corrected for the finished letter. For example, the curves of the O have been straightened to conform to the straightness of other letters.

You will observe that the basic proportions of letters, studied earlier, now become the patterns for the pen to follow. The resulting letters will acquire thicks and thins according to the direction of the line, and the angle at which the pen is held. (See page 31.)

The basic pen strokes illustrated here should be practiced often, for only by constant practice can the student know of the pen's restrictions and possibilities. Due to the tendency of the pen's nibs to catch in the paper when being pushed, strokes should be made toward the writer.

1. Holding a flat cut steel pen at about a 45° angle to the writing line, and without twisting or turning the pen, follow the movement of the wavy line across the paper as in (a) of Fig. 1. Again, holding the pen at the same 45° angle, move it across the paper as in (b). You will note that the thick and thin lines are made from the change in direction of the pen, and never by pressure.

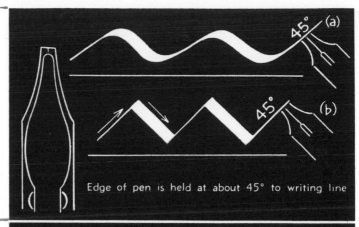

Edge of pen is held at about 45° to writing line

2. In observing the changes made by the changing direction of the pen, one can see that the character of the letters is established by the tool. We can definitely establish the fact that all up strokes are light, and all down strokes are heavy. All horizontal lines are thin. In writing letters with the broad pen, this is accomplished by slightly turning the pen to allow for a thinner line.

Down strokes heavy
Horizontal strokes thin

All up strokes thin   Down strokes heavy

3. The curved parts of the letters are formed in the same manner as described. A good procedure for the student to follow is to place the skeleton forms of the letters under the tracing paper, and with a pen, or a pencil sharpened to a chisel point, trace over the basic forms. Keeping the writing edge of the pen or pencil at the 45° angle, one will find that with a little practice, he will be able to draw a surprisingly good letter.

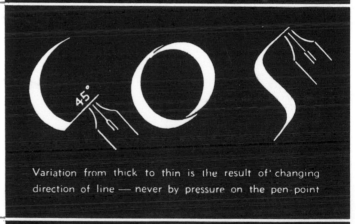

Variation from thick to thin is the result of changing direction of line — never by pressure on the pen-point

4. These letters contain all of the elementary strokes of the Roman alphabet. Any of the capital letters can be assembled from a combination of these strokes. The student should practice these strokes, with both pen and pencil, until he can draw them with ease. By constant comparison with the basic skeleton forms, he will acquire a correct understanding of how letters are formed, and sharpen his perception as to the correct proportions of letters.

These letters contain all the basic strokes

A TYPICAL STROKE IN MAKING LETTERS WITH THE SQUARE CUT PEN

The pen is held in the same position throughout the stroke. Since the line of the curve is constantly changing direction, the thickness of the line will change as the pen follows the arc of the circle.

Beginning at the top edge of the letter, the pen will make a thin line; as it moves around the half circle the line becomes wider. When the pen arrives at the middle part of the curve it makes the widest line at this point. As the stroke continues the line becomes thinner and tapers to a thin line. Curves of similar forms are all made in this manner.

A B C D E F G
H I J K L M N
O P Q R S T U
V W X Y Z &

---

a b c d e f g h i j
k l m n o p q r s
t u v w x y z

SERIFS

One of the distinctive characteristics of the Roman style letters is the serif. The addition of the serif not only adds decoration to the letter, but also aids the eye of the reader in passing from one letter to another.

Although the serif should not be the dominant part of a letter, nevertheless it is the serif that distinguishes many type faces one from the other.

Serifs should be uniform throughout a line of lettering — avoid using a straight serif on one letter with curved or rounded serifs on others.

The models shown here illustrate the various styles used on some of the more popular faces.

The main stems of these letters have been drawn in outline to illustrate that the basic form of the letter is unchanged by the addition of the serif.

(a) shows an interesting experiment. By adding square-shaped serifs to a word, the appearance is materially affected, while the basic forms remain unchanged.

(a)

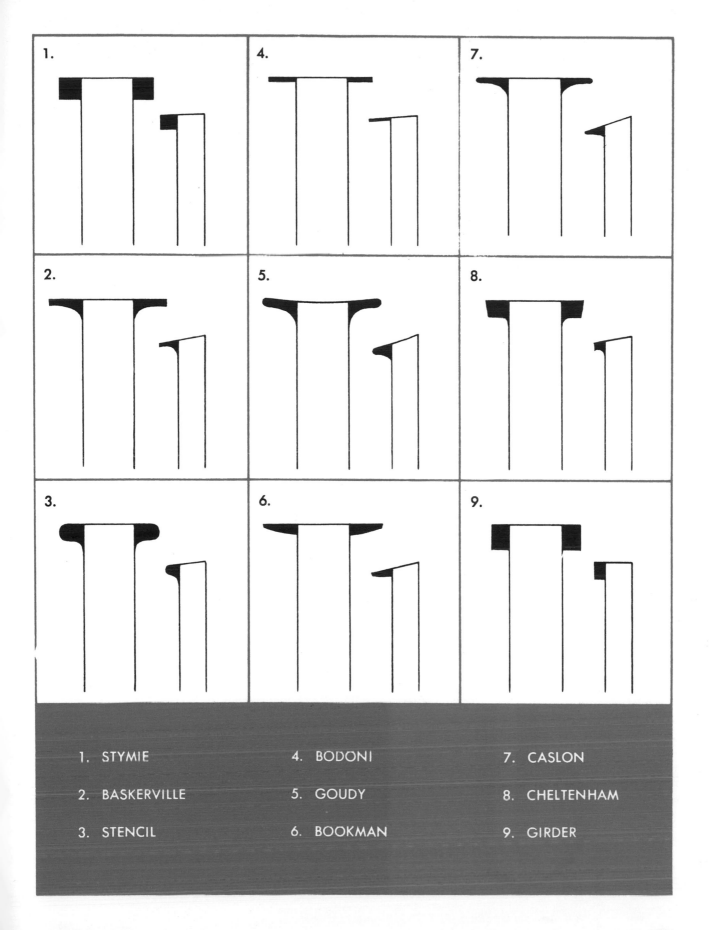

1. STYMIE

2. BASKERVILLE

3. STENCIL

4. BODONI

5. GOUDY

6. BOOKMAN

7. CASLON

8. CHELTENHAM

9. GIRDER

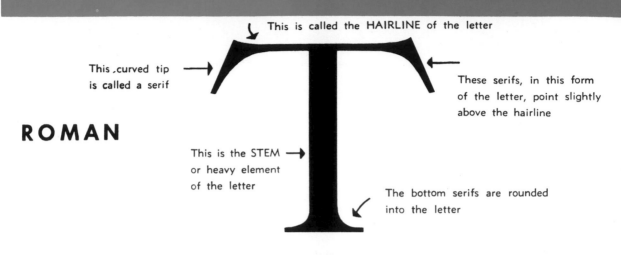

This is called the HAIRLINE of the letter

This curved tip is called a serif →

These serifs, in this form of the letter, point slightly above the hairline

ROMAN

This is the STEM → or heavy element of the letter

The bottom serifs are rounded into the letter

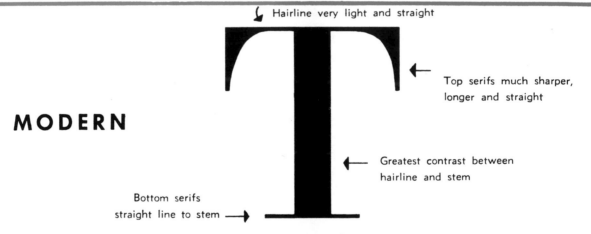

Hairline very light and straight

Top serifs much sharper, longer and straight

MODERN

Greatest contrast between hairline and stem

Bottom serifs straight line to stem →

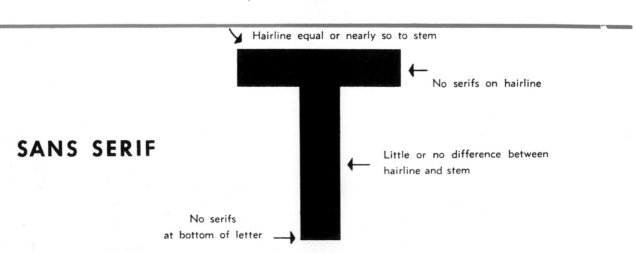

Hairline equal or nearly so to stem

No serifs on hairline

SANS SERIF

Little or no difference between hairline and stem

No serifs at bottom of letter →

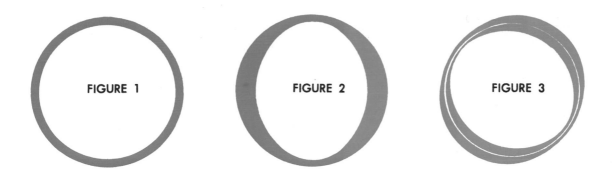

FIGURE 1 FIGURE 2 FIGURE 3

VARIATIONS OF THE BASIC FORMS

For our study of lettering we have assumed the O to be a perfect circle. This form has been recommended as the basic shape of the letters in the circle group. The circle may be the inside or outside dimension, or it may be the center line of a circular form.

Figure (1) shows the basic form built up with the circle as the outside dimension. Figure (2) shows the more conventional type of O, and it also has the circle as its outside form. This conventional form is sometimes made narrower and occasionally widened. The third variation is that of the classic or pen form. In this example (Fig. 3) the circle is the center line of the varying widths of the stroke.

The diagrams A, B and C shown at the bottom of the page, follow the progressive steps in drawing a built-up letter. In diagram A, the shape and modeling of the letter is accomplished by following the basic form with either a square cut pen or a pencil sharpened to a chisel edge.

Diagram B shows the letter in pencil outline preparatory to inking in. The student will observe a radical departure from the pen form in this example. In addition to the drawing of the serifs, the curve of the pen form has been straightened to conform with the conventional form of Fig. (2) shown at top of page.

The third diagram C illustrates the letter carefully outlined by pen and filled in with pen or brush. When outlining a letter, work from the inside of the line out. This method will keep the outside shape of the letter sharp.

ROMAN CAPITALS

The study of the basic sans serif letter proportions, and the distinguishing characteristics of the Roman forms, has prepared the student for study of the complete built-up Roman letters.

The origin of the Roman capitals is from the classical works of the ancient Greeks and Romans. Over a period of time, there have been changes made in the serifs and in the thicks and thins of their strokes. These changes have been made in an effort to improve their readability or because of mechanical demands.

In contrast to preceding discussions on Roman forms, the letters illustrated here are built-up or drawn, rather than written.

The practice of writing the Roman forms is not suggested as a method of execution, but rather for the knowledge gained by knowing their basic construction.

The Roman capitals illustrated on the following pages are accompanied by two diagrams. One diagram shows the basic or skeleton form of the letter, the other the written or pen form.

It is suggested that the student copy these built-up models so that he may acquire a clear and complete understanding of their construction.

These models are to be assumed as a standard or ideal. Though widening and narrowing is occasionally desirable, it will be well to follow the standards illustrated.

A A A

B B B

C C C

D D D

E E E

F F F

G G G

H H H

I I I

41

J J J

K K K

L L L

42

M M M

N N N

O O O

P P P

Q Q Q

R R R

S S **S**

T T **T**

U U **U**

V v V

W w W

X x X

Y Y Y

Z Z Z

& & &

abcdefghi
jklmnopq
rstuvwxyz

In the examples illustrated at the right, note how the serifs and curves have been modified or interpreted from the pen forms.

Basically, the structure of the letter is the same, and it is only in the details that our various type styles differ.

The main difference in character between the Roman types and the modern types is the result of the pen being held at a different angle.

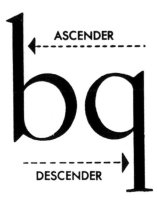

ASCENDER

DESCENDER

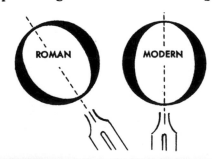

ROMAN   MODERN

ae
CASLON

ae
GARAMOND

ae
BODONI

ROMAN LOWER CASE FORMS

The Roman lower case letters have been established for over 400 years, and they are universally recognized as the types most commonly used in text matter.

The forms are essentially pen forms that evolved naturally from the capitals.

The history and development of these forms is a most interesting one, and many fine books are available on the subject.

The name **lower case** was applied to these letters by printers who kept them in a separate case, usually beneath the case containing the capitals.

The shapes and proportions of the lower case letters follow the same forms as the skeleton sans serif letters illustrated earlier in the book. The letters acquire their character from the broad pen, in the same manner as the Roman capitals.

Since the lower case letters are not as angular in form as the capitals, the natural influence of the pen will be more obvious in the de-

signing and rendering of these forms.

Type designs based on early pen forms were simplified and changed during the built-up process. In drawing built-up letters, the control of the pen is less obvious and more depends upon the skill of the craftsman for his interpretation of the written form.

That the student may understand more clearly the following charts of the lower-case forms, let us construct a letter based on this procedure.

Holding a flat cut pen, or chisel-pointed pencil, at a 45° angle, trace over the basic form of the letter (a). The result will be a written letter with contours and shading resulting from the natural influence of the pen as in (b).

Place this written model (b) under a sheet of transparent paper, and using a pen, or a pencil sharpened to a point, redraw the letter referring to the charts of Roman lower case letters for details of the built-up letters (c).

BASIC
LETTER FORM
(a)

PEN FORM
(b)

BUILT-UP
LETTER
(c)

ROMAN LOWER CASE

The following pages show the complete
Roman lower case forms. As in the pages
illustrating the Roman capitals, each letter is
accompanied by two diagrams — one showing
the basic or skeleton form of the letter,
the other the written or pen form.
The large illustration shows the complete
or built-up model letter.
In studying these forms, note that the t is
shorter than the other ascending letters.
The cross bar crosses on the top line of the
main body of the letters. In drawing the letter
g, the circular form does not go to the
bottom line of the main body as do other letters
of similar construction (b). The descender
of this letter is sometimes drawn out
for decoration purposes.

t g d q
(b)

a a a

b b b

c c c

d d d

e e e

f f f

52

g g g

h h h

i i i

j j j

k k k

l l l

m m m

n n n

o o o

p p p

q q q

r r r

s s S

t t t

u u U

V v V

W w W

X x X

y y Y

z z Z

& & &

your driving

Safer to drive !

You do 80%

Smarter to look

Spring is in the Air!

Examples of typical Roman lettering used in modern advertising.

new character by

A Booth Tarkington

5th Annual Survey

No Other Soap Like Ivory

Colorvision

ROMAN ITALICS

Italic capitals when set in large masses, are difficult to read;
therefore italics are used principally as a lower case alphabet.
The italic lower case letter is a slanting compact letter of
pure pen form. Its beauty comes from the repetition of up and down
strokes, relieved by the curved forms of the serifs.
The basic elements of this letter are the compact oval, the
straight line ending in a curve, and this same line in reverse (a).
These three strokes combined produce most of
the lower case letters in the alphabet.
Example (b) shows how these elements are combined
to produce complete letters.
Italic serifs differ from the Roman serifs in that they are curves,
starting and ending in the same slant as the main stem of the letter.
Some of the letters, notably the f, j, y and r have bulbular
endings that are added purely for design of color (c).
In drawing italic letters, the student has the opportunity
to impart a personal feeling or style to the italic forms that
types rarely achieve. He may give the letters more slant,
or design the forms into a more compact letter. One of the
distinctive characteristics of the italic lower case
is its condensed form.
Usually italic letters lose much of their charm when lettered
in an expanded manner.
Other points that are likely to prove difficult to the student are
illustrated in the charts.

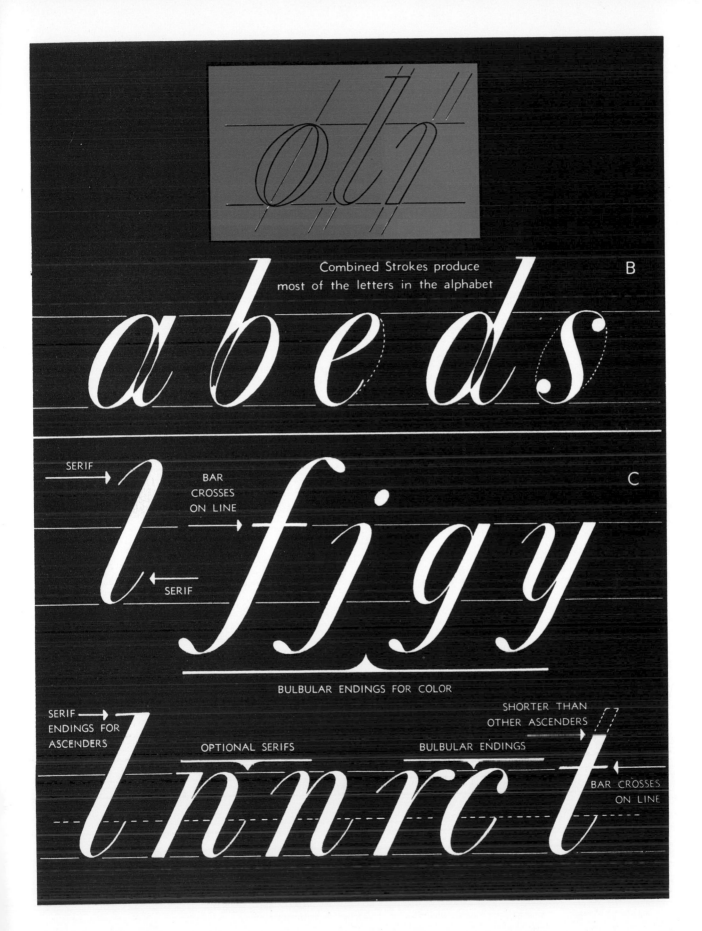

Combined Strokes produce
most of the letters in the alphabet

B

a b e d s

SERIF →

BAR
CROSSES
ON LINE →

C

l fjgy

← SERIF

BULBULAR ENDINGS FOR COLOR

SERIF →
ENDINGS FOR
ASCENDERS

SHORTER THAN
OTHER ASCENDERS →

OPTIONAL SERIFS

BULBULAR ENDINGS

lnnrct

BAR CROSSES
ON LINE ←

Note, in the italic hand lettered examples shown on the opposite page, the introduction of a swash initial (see Page 92), or the accenting of a group ot words in a panel, adds variety and interest to the heading.

Aa Bb Cc Dd Ee

Ff Gg Hh Ii Jj Kk

Ll Mm Nn Oo Pp

Qq Rr Ss Tt Uu

Vv Ww Xx Yy Zz

Thrill your family with

want to look at it...

Security is self-made

*for the 13th Consecutive Year

How To Short-Cut Shortages

After 25_drying

Italic lettering does not conform to any rigid set of rules. There are many styles of this letter, as illustrated above. These letters, though fundamentally alike in construction, vary in weight and slant according to the interpretation of the artist who designs them.

ROMAN NUMERALS

Roman numerals may be classified as
being in two classes — the old-style
figures and lining figures.
The forms of these figures are essentially
the same in both groups, the lining figures
being of equal height, approximately as tall as
the capitals. The old-style figures are of
varying heights. The illustration shows
these differences.
Some types show the old-style cipher as a perfect
circle with uniform weight throughout.
The cipher used in the lining figures
is a condensed O.

795 **5** 2,48

78 68

24 1395 13

67890

OLD ENGLISH

The Gothic black letter, or Old English, is a definite
pen formed letter. It is the simplest of all letters to draw
with a flat cut pen.
This style of letter, though limited in present day usage,
commands attention by its decorative qualities
and even color of line.
Because of our unfamiliarity with these forms,
reading more than a few words is difficult, therefore
these letters are used where ornament is more desirable
than legibility.
Variations can be made in both the lower case and
capital letters. The many varieties of these forms make
the establishment of proportion and any description
of the strokes difficult.
A complete alphabet is shown on page 70. These forms
and their construction can be better understood by tracing
over the patterns of the letters with a square cut pen.
This letter, like the italics, is used mostly in lower case.
Note that angularity and an upright condensed feeling
is characteristic of this style.

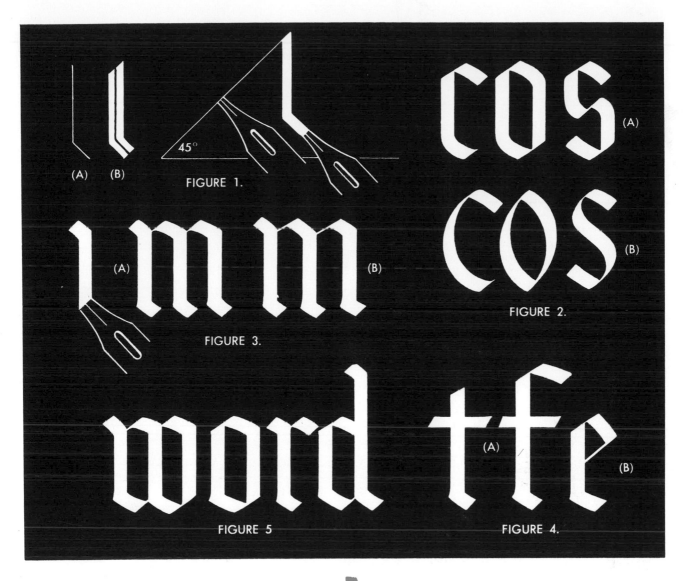

FIGURE 1.

FIGURE 2.

FIGURE 3.

FIGURE 4.

FIGURE 5

1. Holding a square cut pen at an angle of about 45° to the writing plane, and without twisting or changing the position of the pen, trace over line (a). The result will look like (b). This is the main stroke of the lower case letters.

2. You will note that the pen stroke goes abruptly from the thick to the thin part of the letter (a). Individual letters may have a number of interpretations. Each is acceptable if the letter shapes follow the true pen form (b).

3. In drawing these letter forms, allow a little more than the width of the pen stroke (a) within the open letters. Leave about the same amount between individual letters (b). If more than this width is allowed the letters will be too open in appearance.

4. Unlike the Roman letters that we have studied, the cross bars of the f and t are heavy (a). With the exception of the letter e , there are few thin lines in this alphabet (b). Note in Fig. 5, letters are spaced close to accomplish evenness of color.

ABCDEFGHI
JKLMNOPQR
STUVWXYZ

abcdefghij
klmnopqr
stuvwxyz

Excellent examples of Old English used for decorative headings and trade marks.

SCRIPT

The script letter is one of the most exacting
letters to draw. Its forms depend upon good
free-hand drawing, a feeling for good design, and
perfect craftsmanship in its execution. The letter
should be penciled in accurately for all details
before drawing. The curves should be exact and
the slant of the letters uniform throughout. Correct
form in all types of lettering is imperative — in
script it may be said to be exceptionally so.
This alphabet should only be attempted after
practice with the established basic forms.

A B C D E F
G H I J K
L M N O P
Q R S T U
V W X Y Z

a b c d e f g
h i j k l m
n o p q r s
t u v w x y z

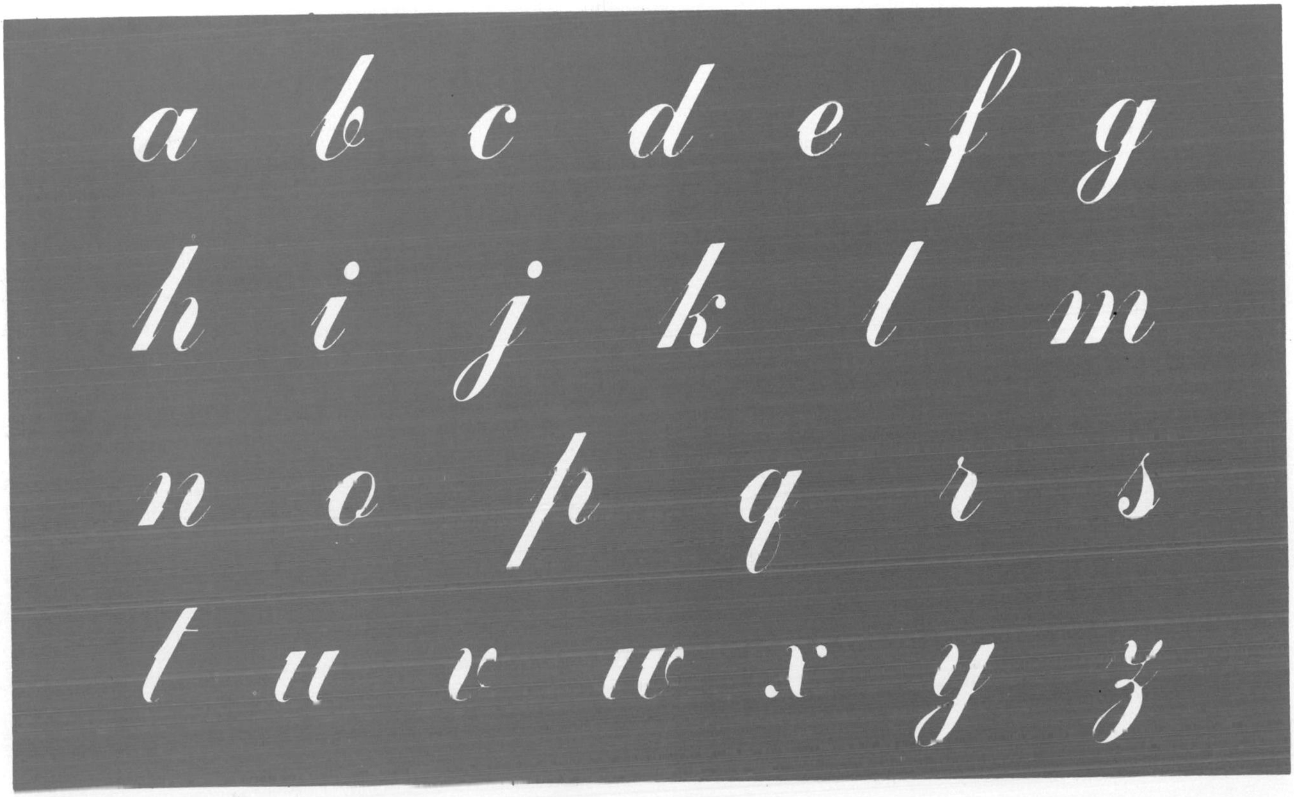

A B C D E F G
H I J K L M N
O P Q R S T U
V W X Y Z &c

This beautiful script alphabet is taken from an English copy book. It is a very
exacting letter, and should be penciled in very accurately before rendering.

a b c d e f g h i j k
l m n o p q r s t u
v w x y z z &Co.

Dreams do come true...

For Quality   Gracious room

Modern   Traditional

Feminine   Style Appeal

Smooth riding

DESCRIPTIVE LETTERING

Hand lettering can be made to harmonize
with a design or it can be used to express
an idea. The lettering artist is not
restricted by the mechanical limitations
of type and he can use any motif
to illustrate the sense of a word. A few
practical considerations are mentioned as a
caution to an overzealous designer.
The style or type of letters used in
a design must be placed and drawn as
carefully as any other element in the
design. The letters should be in harmony
with the subject they illustrate.
The following examples show, rather
than tell, about the possibilities of this
type of letter design.

THÉATRE
MASQUES

Old Fashioned

LeKwangzi

Jiggle FRENCH
TOUCH

DRAWING HINTS

Attention value and interest are often added
to a word or phrase by enclosing them
in a shape or area of design.
These areas are many and varied, and only a few of
the more common ones are illustrated on the
following pages. These diagrams are offered only
as a stimulus to thinking along parallel lines.
The drawing of borders and geometrical shapes
should be done neatly and accurately. The
methods illustrated here should serve as
an aid to correct construction.

Frequently it is necessary to reduce or enlarge the dimensions of an area. To find the second dimension when only one is known we use a method that is known as scaling. This method is explained by the accompanying text and diagram.

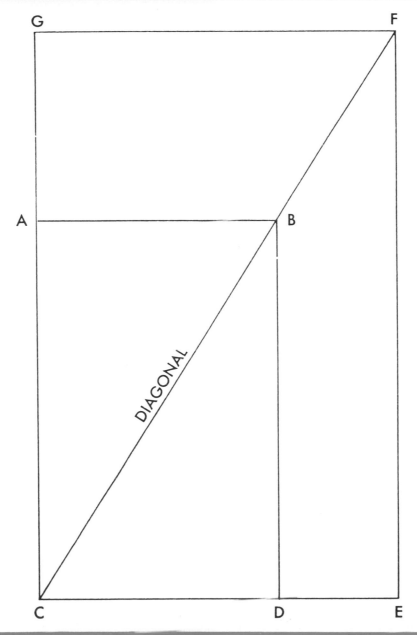

The rectangle ABCD represents an area 2½ x 3⅞ inches which is to be enlarged to 3¾ inches wide. Our problem is to find the height of the area when it is increased in width.

Draw a diagonal through either corner of the rectangle, then draw out the horizontal line CD to any desired length, mark off on this line the enlarged size, which in this case is 3¾ inches. Erect a perpendicular (E) parallel to DB. At the point where this line cuts the diagonal, draw line FG parallel to AB. This rectangle represents the enlarged area. To reduce, reverse the process.

TYPOGRAPHY

This chapter on type measurements grew out of
repeated questions from students regarding type and the
various terms used in type composition.
The text and examples are confined to fundamentals.
They are offered only as introductory remarks
to a study of type faces and typographic procedure.
Type faces may be regarded as a branch
of lettering, for types commonly used in printing
are patterned after letter forms that were
written with pens in early manuscripts.
Variations in the kinds of pens used and in the manner
of using them resulted in many styles of writing.
Basically there are but four letter forms. These forms
are known as Text, Roman, Italic and Script.

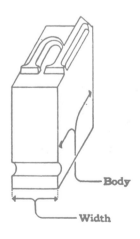

Body

Width

TEXT — When Text types are composed in masses, the lines are difficult to read, and so Text types are rarely used for type masses in printing of a commercial nature. Usage is generally confined to (a) display lines that are brief enough to be readable and that require the decorative quality of the Text letter; (b) religious works in which ecclesiastical character is desired more than readability; (c) formal announcements such as wedding invitations.

ROMAN — This letter form was used in writing early manuscripts and is the form that was carved on the stone panels of Roman buildings. It is legible because of its nature and because it is the familiar letter form in books printed in Latin, English, French, Spanish, Italian, and Portuguese. The Roman form of type is used almost exclusively for the type masses in commercial printing, and is the most generally used form for display heads.

ITALIC — This letter form was used in early informal written manuscripts; but currently, most Italics are sloped modifications of Roman letters and are intended for use as companions of the Roman letters. Italic types are used (a) in the midst of masses of Roman types to emphasize selected words, phrases, or paragraphs; (b) as subheads; (c) as display heads when a decorative or feminine quality is desired.

SCRIPT — This is a variation of the Italic form in which all lower case letters are connected. This form is not believed to be legible in masses, and is used only for occasional display headings and for formal announcements such as wedding invitations.

HOW I
is one to

HOW IS
one to asses

HOW IS O
one to assess

HOW IS ONE
to assess and ev

HOW IS ONE TO
assess and evaluate

HOW IS ONE TO
assess and evaluate a

HOW IS ONE TO ASSESS A
and evaluate a type face in te

TYPE SIZES
AND MEASUREMENTS

Printers do not measure their types or printing materials in inches, but in a unit of measure called a **point.** A point is one-seventy-second of an inch. This unit is used in multiples to measure typographic material. For example, 72 points equal 1 inch, 36 points equal ½ inch, 18 points equal ¼ inch.

The point size is a system for measuring the body of a type, not its face (see Fig. 1).

Not all type faces occupy equal space on their bodies, and two type faces of equal size bodies may have the appearance of two distinct sizes (Fig. 2).

To determine the point size of any type face, choose a word, or phrase, that contains both an ascender, and a descender. Measure from the top of the ascender to the bottom of the descender.

The length of a line of type is called the "measure." The unit for measuring the length of a line of type is called a **pica.** A pica is 12 points or one-sixth of an inch. Therefore, 1 inch contains 6 picas. A line of type that measures 3 inches across is 18 picas wide. Rulers graduated in picas as well as in inches are necessary for measuring type pages. These rulers may be obtained from commercial type houses.

Sizes for newspaper space are designated in columns and agate lines. The width of a column varies in many newspapers. Usually a column will measure 2 inches in width. The depth is designated in agate lines, and there are 14 of these lines to the inch. An advertisement that is 140 agate lines deep will measure 10 inches in depth.

Magazines and business publications almost always designate the page sizes in inches.

The student who hopes to take up layout work must have an understanding of type measurements and type sizes.

Often a layout can be brightened or made more interesting if certain words or phrases are emphasized. Such changes can be made by the use of type in varying sizes and combinations. The examples illustrated show some of these combinations.

A SIMPLE PROCEDURE FOR INVITING ECONOM IC SERVICE IS TO RESTRICT SPECIFICATIONS OF TYPE REQUIRE ments to basic classes and thereby to allow the typographer } Caps / Small caps / Lower case

A simple procedure for inviting economic service is to restrict specifications of type requirements to basic classes and thereby } Italics

In its simple form, Management is an application of METHOD to one's own effort. In its more complex form, Managemen } Small caps for emphasis

In its simple form, Management is an application of *Method* to one's own effort. In its more complex form, Managemen } Italics for emphasis

EFFECTIVE DESIGN—Men and women that are inexperienc ed in designing typographic compositions are disposed to assu } Small cap Subhead

Effective Design — Men and women that are inexperienced in designing typographic compositions are disposed to assu } Italic Subhead

Effective Design—Men and women that are inexperienced in designing typographic compositions are disposed to assu } Bold Subhead

FIGURE 1.

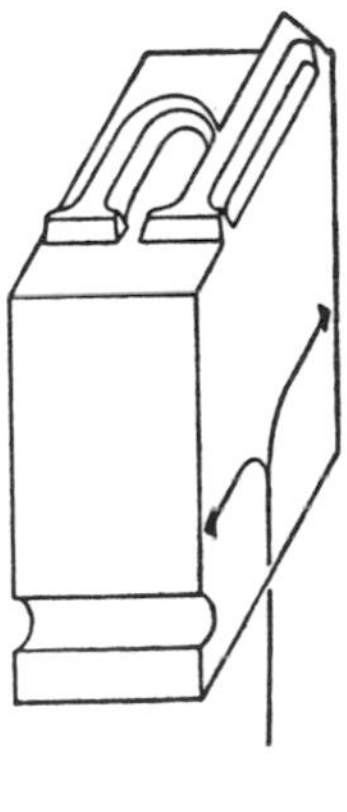

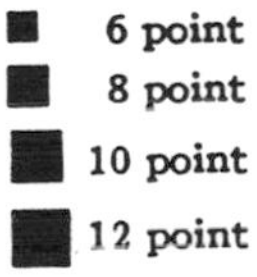

- ■ 6 point
- ■ 8 point
- ■ 10 point
- ■ 12 point

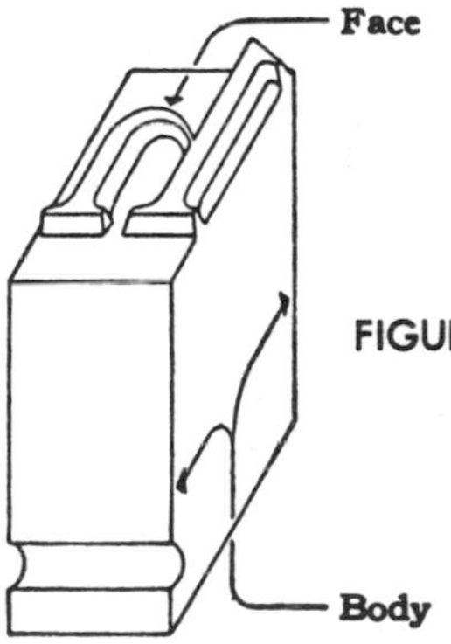

Face

FIGURE 2.

Body

A good axiom to remember is — all display is no display.

BLURB is *unquestionably* the **finest** product of **all time.** It is *wonderful, beautiful, efficient,* and it has that **extra** quality that **only** comes in BLURB. Buy BLURB today. Go to your dealer *now* — at once. Do not **delay**; the demand for BLURB is **tremendous.** *Hurry,* **hurry, HURRY.**

TYPE ALPHABETS

Lettering and type faces have so much in
common that anyone contemplating the study
of lettering must devote some time to the
study of type and type faces.
The following alphabets have been chosen
for their beauty and readability.
For practice trace over these forms with a broad
pencil, sharpened to a chisel point, striving only for
the characteristics of the letter. In doing this you will
acquire a knowledge of a variety of type faces
that will keep your work fresh and interesting.
The differences in the thicks and thins of the modern
types are more extreme than those of the earlier
hand-drawn letters. This development came
about through the desire of printers for
a type which would print much sharper
on the high surfaced printing papers.
Letters from a good type face, such as some of
those shown on the following pages, are
freely copied or adapted, according to
the creativeness of the artist.

FUTURA

A B C D E F G
H I J K L M N O
P Q R S T U V W
X Y Z & ! ?

a b c d e f g h i
j k l m n o p q r
s t u v w x y z

A B C D E F G
H I J K L M N O
P Q R S T U V W
X Y Z & ? !

a b c d e f g h i
j k l m n o p q r
s t u v w x y z

GARAMOND

A B C D E F G
H I J K L M N O
P Q R S T U V W
X Y Z & ? !

a b c d e f g h i
j k l m n o p q r
s t u v w x y z

BODONI

A B C D E F G
H I J K L M N O
P Q R S T U V W
X Y Z & ? !

a b c d e f g h i
j k l m n o p q r
s t u v w x y z

LYDIAN

A B C D E F G

H I J K L M N O

P Q R S T U V W

X Y Z & ! ?

a b c d e f g h i

j k l m n o p q r

s t u v w x y z

A B C D

E I M

O P U V

W &

v w e a e o u

ACTUAL CENTER   OPTICAL CENTER

Avoid placing type or a design in
the actual center of an area. A more
pleasing arrangement is to place the
design at the optical center. This
center is slightly above and to the
left of the actual center.

The top and side margins of a rectangle should be alike in size, the
bottom area, larger.

P. S.

The first consideration for a student in the
study of lettering should be to learn
the basic forms and construction of letters.
We have tried to include only as much information
on each subject as we considered necessary to an
understanding of a basic approach to the subject.
Many readers may consider that the establishment of
rules defeats the principles of good lettering. This
point of view is expected, but if the book enables one
to establish a starting point, then the rules are justified.
It is sincerely hoped that this book will help
the student to a better understanding and
appreciation of good basic letter forms.
We take this opportunity to acknowledge and
thank any source of information that we have
used, either directly or indirectly. Rather than make
disturbing notes of acknowledgment throughout
the book, we are listing some of these sources
and recommending them for further study.

BOOKS SUGGESTED FOR FURTHER STUDY

★　★　★

EDWARD JOHNSON
Writing, Illumination and Lettering

TOMMY THOMPSON
How to Render Roman Letter Forms

RUSSELL LAKER
Anatomy of Lettering

F. W. GOUDY
The Alphabet

A. J. FAIRBANK
A Manual of Handwriting

OSCAR OGG
An Alphabet Source Book

★　★　★

Many people have been cooperative in lending assistance to the author in assembling this book.
I would like to acknowledge the kindness of the S. D. Warren Company of Boston for their permission to use excerpts from the excellent pamphlet entitled "Printing Types and Typography".
I would also like to acknowledge the cooperation of Mayer Goldman, whose help and comments have encouraged me in compiling this book.

R. D. B.